ZOOM CONNECT 2020

USER'S GUIDE

Fast and Easy Way to Master the Zoom Communication and advance Online Meeting, Videos Conferences and Webinars ideals with Tips and Tricks

DAVID

GREAT

Copyright

Printed in the United States of America
© 2020 by David Great

Churchgate Publishing House

USA | UK | Canada

Table of Contents

Chapter 5

Chapter 6

Why This Guide?

If you need a regular Virtual meeting that does everything that the top of the line, Zoom does for four times less the stress and safe unsual time of going to a particular location for the meeting which make it your best bet. However, if You need a comprehensive guide to walk you through the essential settings, configurations and numerous handy tips, tricks, hidden features of Zoom Video Communications, then this guide is for you. It provides an insight into the basic functions of the Zoom such as video-telephony and online chat services through a cloud-based peer-to-peer platform software, etc to advanced functions such as creating Advanced teleconferencing, telecommuting, distance or online education, advanced gestures, setting up advanced security and techniques to master various advanced settings to safeguard your Zoom Meeting and increase productivity.

This book also gives you insight to how you can reach other people in and offshores, you should purchase and seamless techniques to connect with Zoom Community for maximum performance.

Chapter 1

INTRODUCING ZOOM

THE BASIC

Zoom Video Communications Inc. is an American communications Technology Company whose headquarter is located in San Jose, California. It provides video telephony and online chat services through a cloud-based peer-to-peer platform software. It is used for teleconferencing, telecommuting, distance or online education, and other social relations. Zooms' business generally focuses on providing an easy to use platform which is cost-effective and includes minimizing computational costs at the infrastructural level and having a high degree of user efficiency.

Zoom is a cloud-based video conferencing platform you can use to have a virtual meeting with others using video or audio or both along with chats. It allows us to record such meeting sessions so you can view or transfer it later. The best video conferencing apps can do more than just enabling a virtual face-to-face meeting. They let you show what's on your screen to participants on the call, pass control of the meeting to another person, and record the call as a video. Zoom Web conferencing service offers all these features and more, some of them may seem hidden as options in advanced menus.

Many companies, firms, or organizations use the Zoom Cloud Meeting platform for conferences mainly since the outbreak of the Nobel virus to communicate the way forward. Zoom meetings are held in the zoom meeting room. A-Zoom Meeting Room is the physical hardware that lets you host, join, or schedule zoom meetings. Zoom Rooms require an additional subscription other than the regular zoom subscription and better solution for larger companies.

It permits to interact with co-workers and employers during meetings virtually. Zoom makes telecommunicating appear more visual as it enables you to feel connected. Zoom has become an essential tool for small, medium, and large teams that must keep in touch and continue their daily workflows with minimum distractions.

Zoom lets the guest of a meeting have a video call with or without the host being present. Small groups sometimes like this option because they can have a few minutes of fun before the meeting officially starts. You can decide to create a virtual waiting room where participants remain on hold until you bring them in at the same time or one after the other.

You can join a Zoom Meeting or Webinar without a Webcam, but you will not be able to transmit a video of yourself. You will be able to listen and speak during the meeting, share your screen, and view other participants' webcam videos.

Zoom allows you to record your web conferencing calls as videos, a useful feature for sharing the meeting with people who may have missed it or for reviewing purpose.

When you record, you must decide whether to use the local or cloud option. Local storage means storing the video file yourself, either on your computer or in another storage space like a folder or an external device. Cloud storage is for paying members only; Zoom helps you store your video in its cloud storage. Different account types come with varying amounts of storage.

When setting up a Zoom Room, you need a computer to synchronize and run Zoom Meetings and a tablet for guests to launch the Zoom Meetings. You also need a microphone, camera, speaker, and one HDTV monitors to display remote meeting participants, an HDMI cable to share computer screens on display, and an internet cable for your connection.

You will need to download "Zoom Conference Room" on the in-room computer and "Zoom Room Controller" for your connecting device in the zoom meeting room. You can then synchronize those rooms to your shared calendar so that every employee can see which meeting rooms are available. Zoom offers a secure, cost-effective, and easy-to-use platform for messaging, cloud meetings, conferencing and Webinars, Zoom is the business communication tool of businesses globally. Zoom video conferencing and Zoom Rooms feature has solidly established Zoom as one of the world's most popular collaborating platforms for training, conference, board meetings, and meeting rooms for businesses of all sizes.

FEATURES OF ZOOM

ZOOM CLOUD MEETINGS

Zoom Cloud Meetings is one powerful online meeting solution available today. Zoom provides communications software that incorporates cloud video conferencing, online meetings, chat, and remote collaboration in one platform. The Zoom Meeting is a core feature of the Zoom suite because it enables teams worldwide to work effectively by providing a innovative communication platform and collaboration tools that bring people closer together. Zoom is hugely scalable and can be used by individuals, small or large teams, all the way up to full participation in a live event, conferences with hundreds of participants and thousands of viewers.

Zoom can be instantly activated on Zoom's cloud, making the software preferred by IT experts. On the Zoom platform, video, voice, and any content shared all run securely on the cloud.

MEETING/ EVENTS THAT YOU CAN HOST USING THE ZOOM PLATFORM

- Collaborative working
- Training sessions
- Presentations
- Sales meetings
- Board meetings
- Technical support
- Conferences

- Live chats
- Live streaming.

FEATURES OF ZOOM CLOUD MEETINGS

HD audio and video conferencing: Zoom has high definition audio and video features, allowing you to have communications that are crisp, clear, and easily understood when using Zoom.

Flexible screen views: You can switch lights between full screen and gallery view to easily organize your conference settings as you want them.

High-quality recordings: Record any meeting or conference in high-quality MP4 and MP4A formats.

Compatibility: No matter which device or operating system you are using, Zoom will performs very well. A standard experience across devices removes frustrations, no time lost, and no sophisticated training, users can concentrate on getting the business done.

Dynamic voice detection: Makes it easy to determine who is speaking, even if lots of participants are speaking simultaneously.

Powerful collaboration tools: Zoom has a digital Whiteboard feature that allows you to draw and make notes in real-time, which can then be shared with other participants.

Screen sharing: Zoom's interface makes screen sharing a simple process. Whether you want to share your desktop, display a visual presentation, or share an entire video, Zoom screen sharing is easy and effective.

Remote access: One of the most useful features of Zoom for co-working is the ability to allow remote access to your device.

Easy content sharing: From sharing documents on your desktop to playing a presentation video saved on your device to sharing images saved in third-party tools like Dropbox or Google Drive, Zoom makes it easy to share content from multiple sources during the meeting.

Interoperability with H.323 and SIP conference systems: You can effortlessly connect Zoom with your existing conference room system hardware. Zoom works efficiently with video endpoints from other major conference room systems, including Lifesize, Polycom, and Cisco.

Easy initiation: Meetings can be initiated instantly or scheduled ahead of time with the integration of calendar and reminders sent beforehand.

Host controls: Zoom allows the meeting host to have full control over the meeting, determining who joins the meeting and what they can do during the session.

Easy invites: Each meeting is provided with a unique meeting ID, so you can easily invite new participants by sending them the meeting ID, and they can join the meeting with just a click.

The ZOOM ROOM

A zoom room is a conference room ready cloud-based communication technology solution. Zoom is a video conferencing software that will allow you to have a meeting face-to-face with video and audio as well as a chat. A-Zoom room runs on cutting edge software available for "Mac and Windows systems." This technology saves costs for users by eliminating the need for expensive and sometimes cumbersome hardware based on video conference and telepresence technologies. Zoom rooms provide the flexibility of sharing crisp, highest-quality videos, screen content, and voice communication in any size room or meeting space. Users may join zoom meetings or host instant meetings from any zoom room system, and users may establish a calendar integration to schedule meetings for a zoom meeting as well. Users may deploy multiple high definition displays and state-of-the-art cameras and audio systems to achieve a communication center customized to fit. They may best take advantage of the space they create and connect smart board technology with zoom room for touch displays. All of these are controlled from an intuitive easy to use tablet application. Use your zoom room and your meeting space to create and organize and achieve your goals. Zoom rooms are just one way there, and zoom video communications are working to keep people and teams connected with seamless communication quality. Zoom Rooms are the hardware and software answers from Zoom designed to help businesses create open meeting rooms. You can access one-click meeting starts, HD video and audio, and all the latest technology from Zoom in a conference room. Building the perfect conference room is comfortable with Zoom Rooms, and you can even access a range of different hardware options to suit your choices.

Zoom offers four pricing options (Zoom Room subscription not included)

FREE ZOOM: This option is free. You can host a limitless number of meetings. Group meetings with multiple participants are sealed at 40 minutes in length, and sessions can't be recorded.

ZOOM PRO: This option costs $14.99/£11.99 per month for the meeting host. It allows hosts to create personal meeting IDs for hosting Zoom Meetings, and it permits meeting recording to the cloud or your device, but it peaks group meeting durations at 24 hours.

ZOOM BUSINESS: This rank costs $19.99/£15.99 per month for meeting hosting. It lets you marque Zoom meetings with empty URLs and company trademarks or logo, and it offers transcripts of Zoom meetings recorded in the cloud and dedicated customer support.

ZOOM ENTERPRISE: This rank costs $19.99/£15.99 per month and per meeting and is meant for businesses with 1,000 or more employees. It offers limitless cloud storage for recordings, a customer success manager, and a rebate on webinars and Zoom Rooms.

FEATURES OF A ZOOM ROOM

- Conference room connectors.
- HD video and audio.
- One-CLICK meeting join.
- Powerful built-in security.
- One-click wireless sharing.
- Co-annotation whiteboards.
- Range of rooms of all sizes.

- ➢ Scheduling displays.
- ➢ Remote management and software provisioning.
- ➢ Room and location hierarchies.
- ➢ Role-based administration.

ZOOM WEBINARS

Zoom Video Webinars allow you to host meetings with about100 participants who you can interact with, and 1,000 view-only members. Webinars are easy to set up with branded emails and registration forms available. Features include live broadcasting, to event assistance from Zoom specialists, and even reporting and analytics.

ZOOM WEBINARS FEATURES

- ➢ Auto-generated transcripts.
- ➢ On-demand or scheduling webinars.
- ➢ HD video and audio for up to 100 participants.
- ➢ Reporting and analytics on attendees.
- ➢ Live broadcasts via social media channels and YouTube.
- ➢ Event support from the Zoom Team.
- ➢ Host controls like mute/unmute.
- ➢ Q&A and polling features.
- ➢ Hand-raising activity option.
- ➢ Instant chat for participants and host.

ZOOM CHAT

Zoom Chat is included with your Zoom Meetings agreements. Designed to keep teams connected during a meeting, Zoom Chat ensures that you can reach your units with a quick instant messaging, and integrations with all your preferred tools. A brilliant search tool is built-in so that you can choose between one-on-one and group chat too. Starred channels and contacts make it easy to stay focused, while status menu features show you who is online.

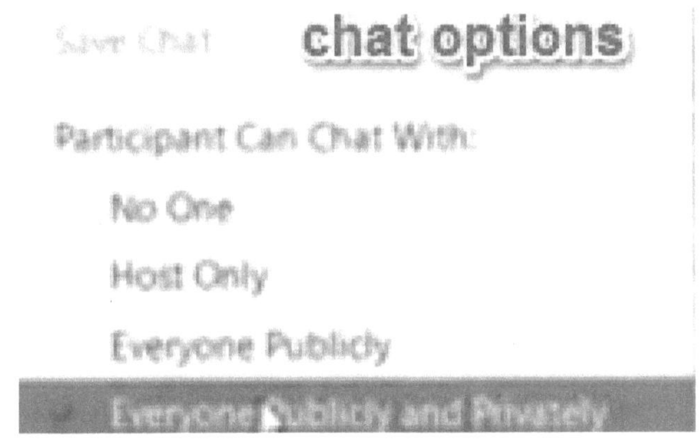

Features include:

- ➢ One-on-one or group chat.
- ➢ Status and presence indicators.
- ➢ Archiving and security authentication.
- ➢ Quick search functionality.
- ➢ Calendar integrations.
- ➢ Mobile and desktop access.

> Settings and notifications to help control the platform.

ZOOM PHONE

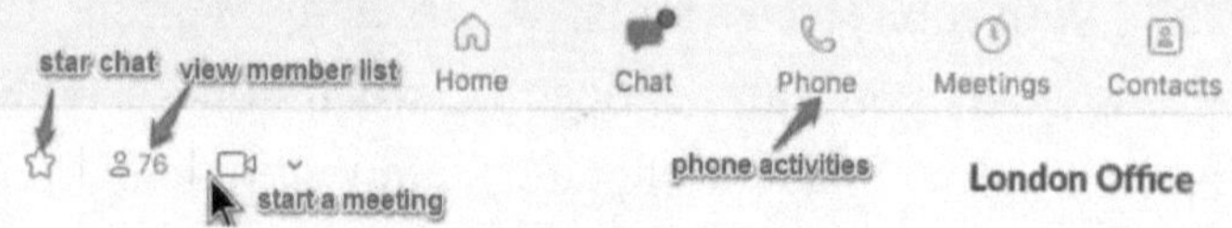

Zoom Phone is the cloud phone system from Zoom, providing businesses with an all-in-one platform for business, voice, and collaborating. You can access the features of a standard traditional phone features.

- Intelligent call routing.
- Integrations with Microsoft and Google.
- Voicemail and call recordings.
- Secure and clear audio.
- Standard-based endpoints interoperability.
- One-click meetings or calls join.
- Cloud saving mode.
- Dashboards to monitor call.

Chapter 2

WHY ZOOM CLOUD MEETING

1. **Zoom is simple to set up and use**: it's one click to start or join any meeting, and Zoom provides secure collaboration and participant controls. You do not need an "IT Team" to roll out and manage Zoom. **Modern communications for your team members.** You can get your entire team on video, up to 100 participants', or to have a quick one-on-one meeting.

3. **Four-in-one benefits (platform for meetings, phone, webinars & chat):** Zoom offers a very wise resource with a single answer for conferences, webinars, telephone, and chat. Zoom continues to update its platform to meet growing business needs, so you don't ever have to worry about finding another communications platform.

4. **Connect via desktop clients, browsers, conference rooms & mobile devices:** Zoom has the best flexibility and simplicity than any other conferencing software. Zoom works in a seamless manner across all operating systems — PC, Mac, Linux, iOS, and Android — so you aren't locked into specific devices.

5. **Zoom has the best value and returns on investment:** We know how important it is to get more done quickly and build relationships through face-to-face interaction. Zoom helps you get connected with various video communications capabilities packed into one low monthly price. Its integration with Google and Microsoft will streamline your meetings, and the App Marketplace has over 200 integrations with leading apps like Slack and PayPal.

6. **Easy:** You have to click on a Zoom link in an invitation, and it will launch your meeting. If you don't have the Zoom app installed, it will prompt you to

download and install it. It's fast and easy, and even the least tech-canny can handle zoom.

7. **Accessible:** You can also use it on any device. It works on your laptop, iPad, iPhone, desktop, or android device. That means pretty much anyone can use it anywhere.

8. **Affordable and reliable:** Zoom is free to use, not just for joining meetings. You can actually host Zoom meetings for free. A load of companies is using Zoom to stay connected and updated, keeping their teams productive.

9. **Fun:** Zoom is really pretty fun. You might think those types of features are totally unnecessary, and you'd be right. Zoom is packed with great features that give you the grace to do as you wish, like the background feature, the mute option, the waiting room, and so on. Zoom delivers a very sensational video conferencing. The video quality is excellent, and the audio comes through clearly. You can share multiple screens and use whiteboard functions to annotate projects.

10. **Zoom Meetings Review Benefits**: One of the most significant benefits of Zoom is how accessible technology is. Setting up a Zoom Meeting is as simple as clicking on an invitation link to launch the app or prompt users to install the interface. There's no need for mass provision solutions because the interface is lightweight and straightforward on both mobile and desktop devices. Zoom offers very-fast functionality, with high-quality audio and video at every price-point.

11. **Zoom Security:** Zoom is making changes to its security strategy and implementing new features. All meetings now require host permission and a password to join.

12. **Excellent support:** Zoom offers very active user support to serve companies and users around the world.

13. **Scheduling:** Zoom allows you to schedule meetings in advance from your Zoom app, which you can connect to a range of other calendars, including those from Google and Microsoft.

14. **Advanced features:** Another benefit of Zoom is that it's constantly updating and improving what users can do with their technology. Virtual backgrounds allow you to get rid of the boring meeting room in the background of your call. Even touch-up functions to enhance beauty for those who are worried about wrinkles.

ZOOM EXCITING FEATURES

- Scheduling services with Outlook and Google.
- Built-in recording and transcripts tools.
- Team chats both for groups and one-on-one messaging.
- Access to other features like webinars, chats, and phone.
- Easy adoption with Web RTC technology.
- Join from anywhere on any device.
- Access robust security solutions throughout.
- Screen sharing built-in tools.
- HD video and very clear audio calls.
- Secured with role-based user permissions.

Chapter 3

TIPS AND TRICKS FOR EVERY USER ON ZOOM MEETING

It doesn't matter if you work remotely; if you work from home or work at bitch side, you can use video conferencing to connect with others. The tips and tricks on zoom meeting platforms will make you a pro.

- To stop every interrupting background noise, press "Alt + M" on your keyboard to mute all.
- To hide floating control panel, tap on "More Icon" (...), then a drop-down menu will display, in here click on the "Hide floating meeting controls" or press "(Ctrl + Alt + shift + H)" on your keyboard.
- To get back to the menu, select Escape (Esc) on your keyboard.

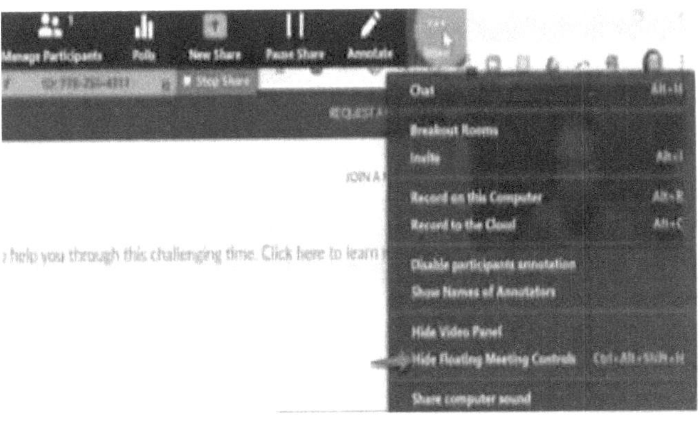

- Under the settings, there are two essential functions that you should take control of. One is your video; under the "video settings" always turn off video when joining the meeting by default, even if you are the host or joining someone else's meeting, so that you can initiate the video when you are ready.

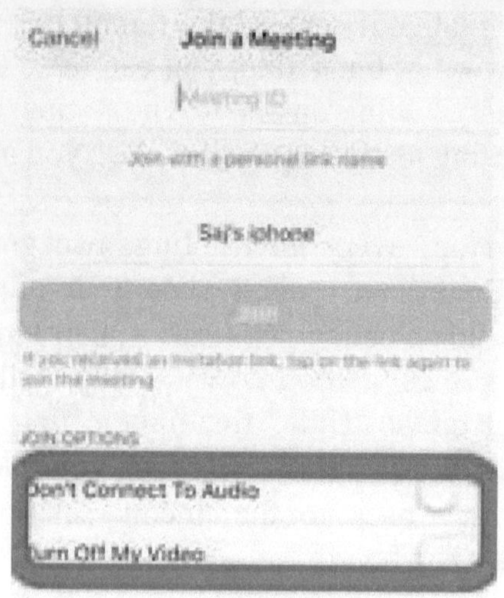

- Next is "Virtual background," go to your settings and select a virtual background from the default images or video background in the zoom app so that you do not have to care so much about what's going on behind you. You can also upload your images with your brand or name on it.

- For your scheduling or calendar features, download "Calendar Add-On for Google and Microsoft," this will gives you the option to schedule a meeting or start a meeting session immediately. It also has the option to start the meeting with your video off or ON.

- Zoom has an exciting bonus called "Make it a Zoom Meeting." With a click on it, the calendar will generate a meeting link, meeting ID, One-tap Mobile info, Dial by your location details that your guest is going to need to join the meeting. Now when it's time for the session, all you need to do is click on join zoom meeting. It will be launch.
- Click On the "Floating control menu," the New Share and Pause share options will display. The new share option allows you to go to another place on your computer where you can find the file or document or images or whatever object you would like to share with your guest without seeing you select or look for your folder. To go back to the web, click New Share, select the web video, and click share.
- For the pause share option, you can use (Alt + P) to leave your guest viewing a particular screen while you go on to another screen to search for something. When done, click on it again to resume share.
- The "Floating control menu," the floating control menu has an option called "Annotate option," which is the last option before "More." The "Annotate" gives you a variety of ways to highlight things on your screen.

ZOOM KEYBOARD SHORTCUTS

Zoom permits the use of various shortcut keys during Zoom meetings to access features or change settings quickly.

These are some of the shortcut keys:
- Alt + A or Command (#) + Shift + A: Mute or unmute audio
- Alt + M or Command (#) + Control + M: Mute or unmute all except the host
- Alt + S or Command (#) + Control + S: Start screen sharing
- Alt + R or Command (#) + Shift + R: Start or stop local recording
- Alt + C or Command (#) + Shift + C: Start or stop cloud recording
- Alt + P or Command (#) + Shift + P: Pause or resume recording
- Alt + F1 or Command (#) + Shift + W: Switch to active speaker view in video meeting.
- Mute and unmute with the space bar.

Chapter 4

HOW TO DOWNLOAD ZOOM APP ON LAPTOP

STEPS

- On your browser, go to the Google search menu and type in zoom download.

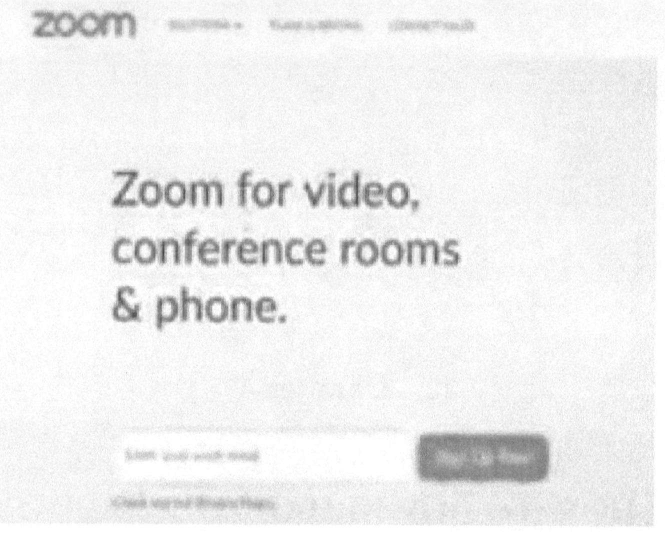

- It will load different download options from various website,
- Click on Download Center –Zoom
- When the download center opens,   click on Download,
- Then choose the right folder where you want your zoom app downloaded to, click save and allow to download.
- Scroll down on the download center page, look for Zoom Client for Meetings and download it.

- When the Zoom App download is complete, go to the folder where you downloaded it to and install it, it's easy and fast.
- When the installation is complete, click on the zoom app on your desktop to open it and sign up
- Click on "Sign Up", you will have to fill in your email and password

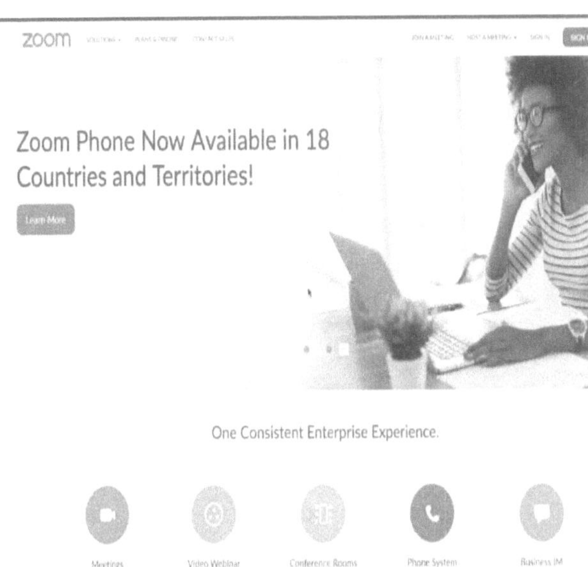

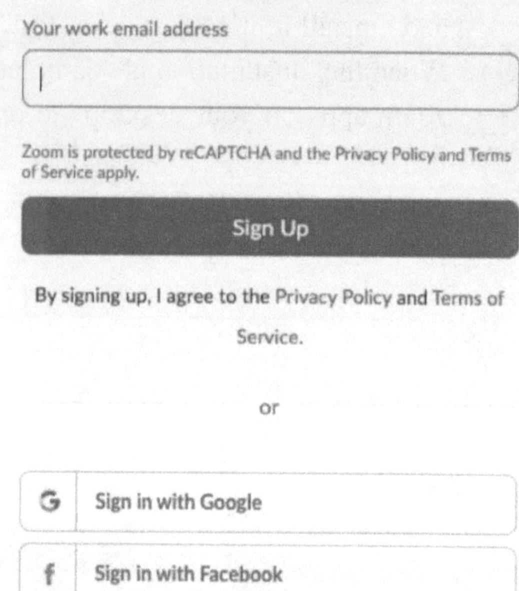

- You will now receive an activation SMS via the email account you entered, open the email and click on activate.

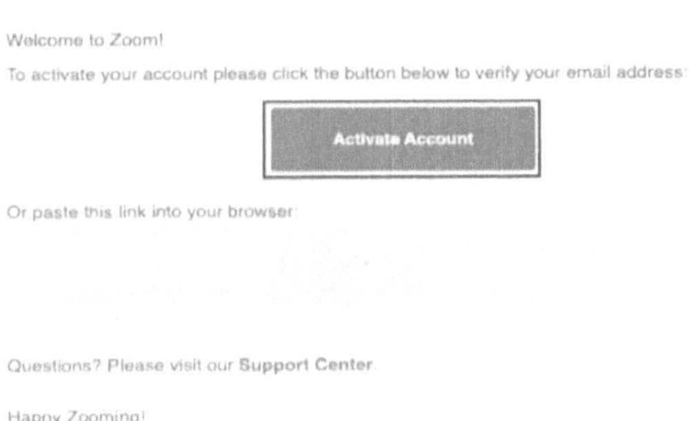

- To finish creating your Zoom account, enter your first name, last name and a password. Make sure your password meets the required perimeters, when done filling in the details click "continue."

- Next you can invite your colleagues to join your meeting by entering their email addresses.

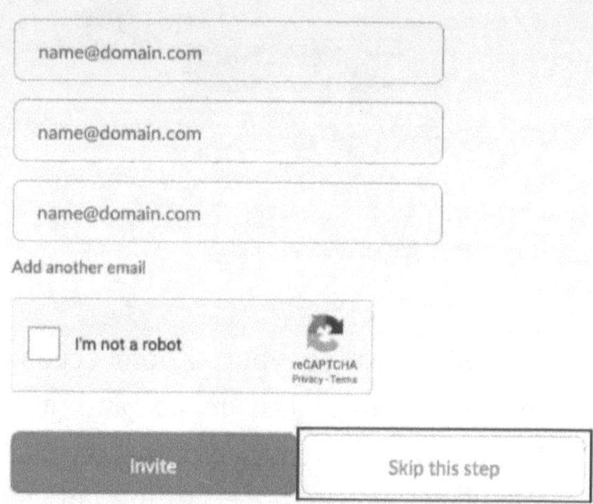

- Or you can click on "Skip this step" and start hosting your first meeting.
- When you click the skip icon another window opens, there you can click on "start meeting now" to host your meeting in your personal meeting room.

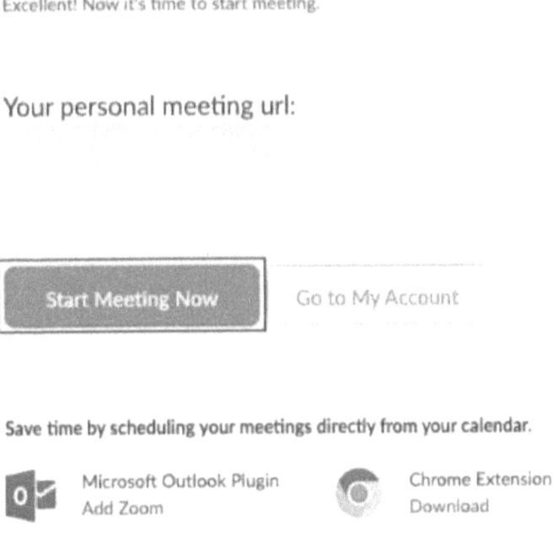

- From that meeting hosting window you click to invite guest to your meeting, by sending them the meeting URL or ID.

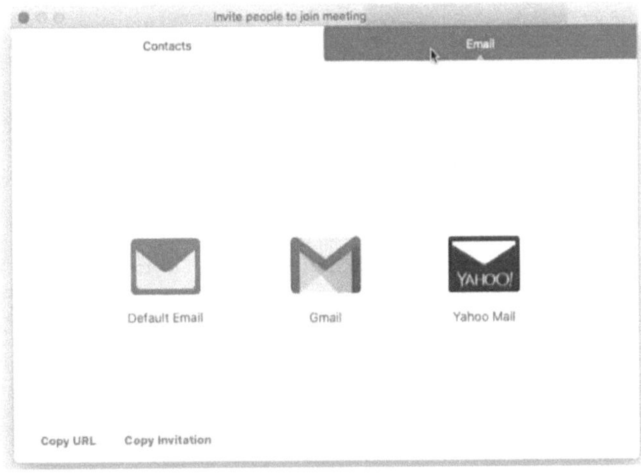

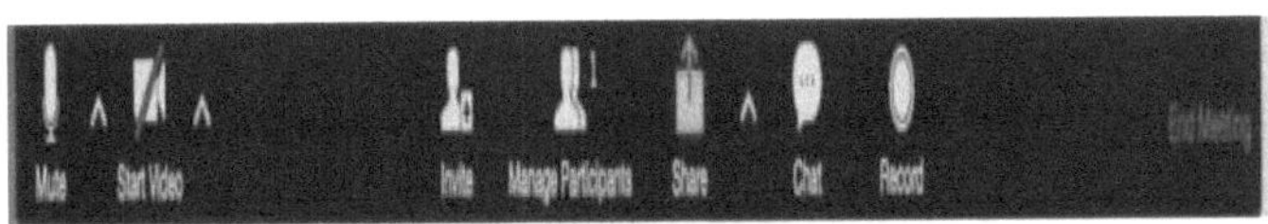

HOW TO USE ZOOM'S DESKTOP APP

Zoom introduces a modern looking field that improves ease of viewer's client software. Its puts more of the tools that you need at your fingertips.

Steps in using Zooms desktop App

> From the home screen you can start a new meeting instantly.

> Click the New meeting Icon, then click on the dropdown menu to choose whether to have the video on or off by default once joined
> And choose whether to use your personal meeting ID.

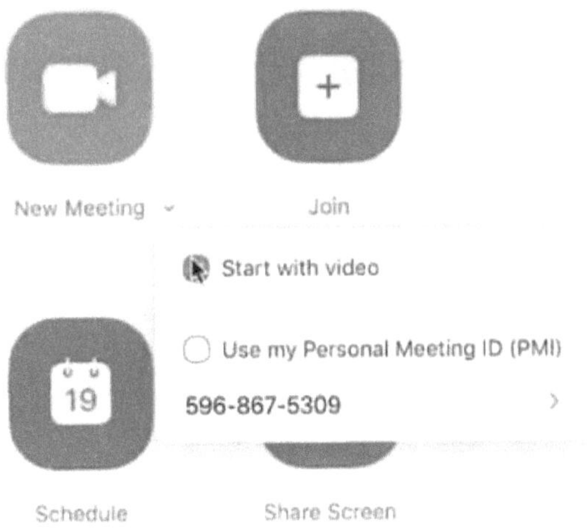

- ➤ You can also use the home screen to join another person's meeting by Meeting ID or Personal Link Name [Meeting Name].
- ➤ Schedule a new meeting for the future by clicking on the Schedule or calendar icon
- ➤ Initiate screen   sharing in a   Zoom   room by clicking on the share screen icon.
- ➤ Switch to the chat screen to keep the conversation going between meetings
- ➤ Chat one-on-one or create a public or private channel for your team to collaborate and share file.
- ➤ Click [+] to start a new chat, create a new channel or Join a channel.

➤ You can also edit or delete a post or chat if you are the   one that   sent it.

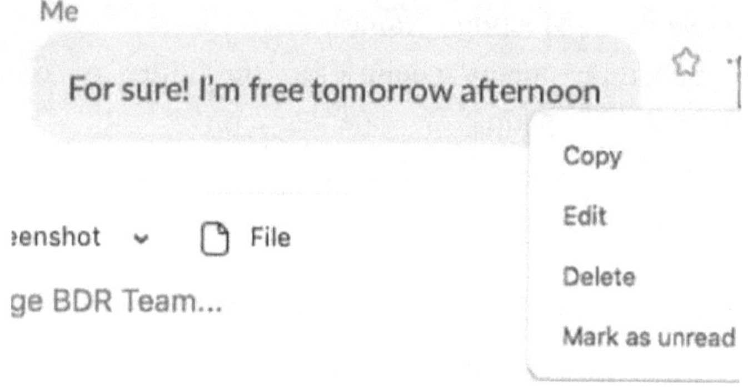

➤ At the bottom of the screen, use the built in screen   shot to capture   and annotate on screenshots.

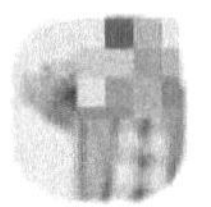

> Upload files and access your Emoji and gifts library.
> Look to the top to star the chat as a favorite.
> View the channels member list.
> Start a meeting, open the chat on a separate window or view info.
> Use the info menu to show channel member details.

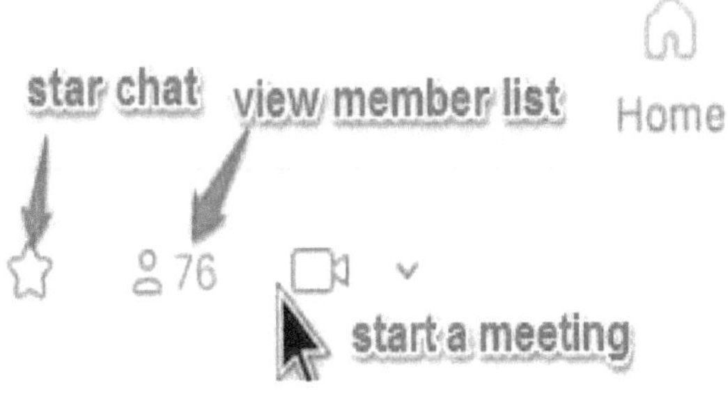

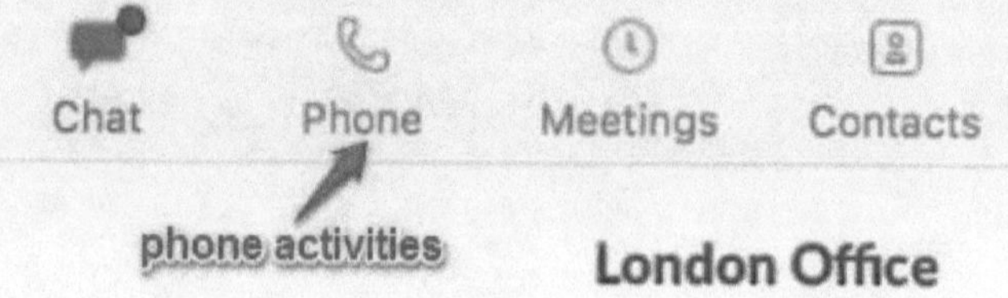

- ➢ Access images and files shared in the chat history and prioritize messages.
- ➢ The phone tab becomes available when you subscribe to zoom voice.
- ➢ Zoom voice has all of your business phone system features and capabilities; you'll find your call history, voicemail and the dial pad to make calls.
- ➢ Access the meeting screen to view up-coming and recorded meeting or schedule a new meeting.
- ➢ Click the meeting icon to start or join a meeting, copy the invitation, edit the meeting settings, delete the meeting or show the meeting invitation.
- ➢ Click the zoom channel screen to view contacts and channels.
- ➢ On the channel screen, click the [+] button to add contacts by email address, create a new channel, join a channel or add an app.

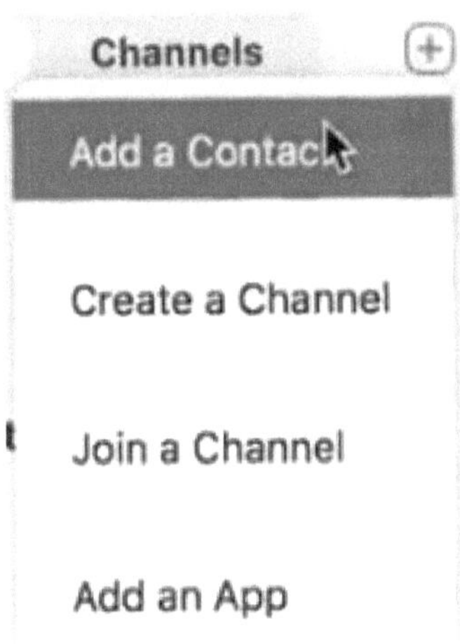

➢ Contacts can be managed by departments or work group by the account owner or administrator through iammanagement@zoom.us.

➢ Click your profile picture at the right corner of the screen to view and edit the personal note others will see when they contact you.

➢ Access the zoom client software settings.

➢ Change your availability status and more.

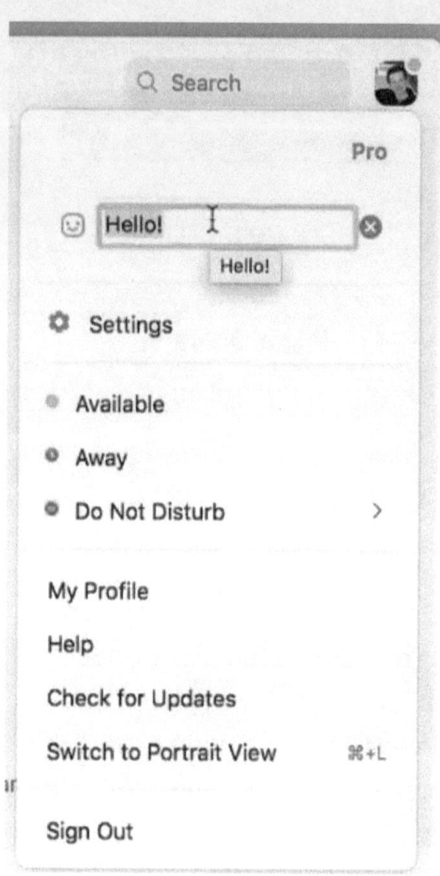

HOW TO USE ZOOM FOR MEETINGS AND VIDEO CONFERENCING

In this session you can use zoom to set up your lectures and video conferences. Zoom is an excellent platform to host online video conferences. Even if you are not a teacher, the zoom is a very robust yet light application where you can set up your video conference in minutes; people will be able to join your meetings by clicking on your link, and an options such as sharing your screen, sharing your video camera and also enabling chats pop up.

STEPS
- The first thing you want to do is go ahead and go to zoom and click on sign up to have your zoom account
- Once you enter your email, click the sign-up, then you will receive an activation or confirmation email on the email account you signed up with
- Click activates account to activate your zoom account, and your zoom account will be ready for use
- Then, create your password and enter your name
- Now once your account is set-up, you're going to be doing a lot with the key app.
- On your account, go to the top and click host a meeting

- A drop-down menu will pop up with options, choose from one of the options displayed in the drop-down menu. You'll be redirected to a new page site downloading the application automatically, and the app will be install. It is a very light application, and it will not take up too much space and do not require intense computing power.

- At the bottom part of the "Zoom Screen," you will find the entire menu options to turn on and off your microphone and your video Camera.
- To change the camera or microphone settings, click on the arrow (^).
- Then choose any options and in the settings change the different settings you have for the webcam and microphone you are using in terms of ratio, resolution, and all that.)

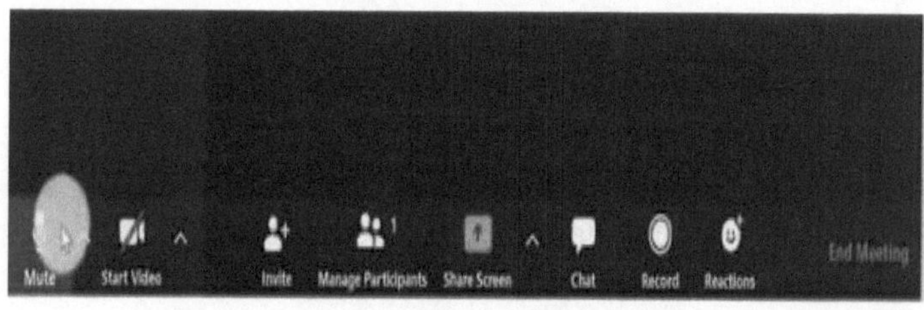

- Now once you have your microphone and video set up, you can invite people to a meeting
- Now there's different ways you can invite people, you can email them, but a preferred way is to click on copy my url, which gives you a url that you can automatically send to people.

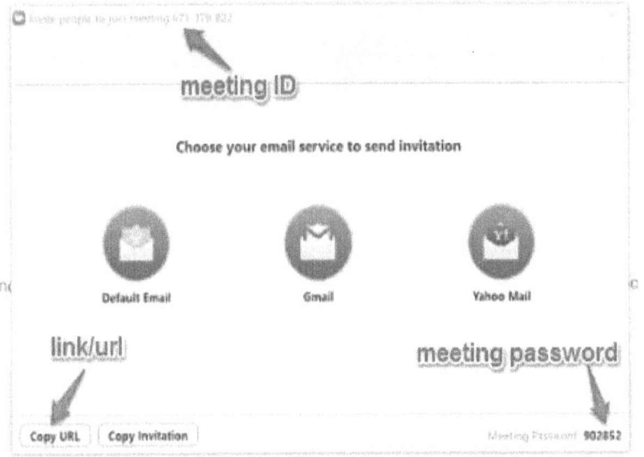

- If the people you send the "url" paste it on their browser, it's going to execute the zoom launch, and they'll be joining the meeting right away.
- Now once you have people invited to your meeting session you can see who is in the conference by clicking on manage participant. Once you tap on manage participant, a bar loop appears on the right, side of the Zoom screen with an options of meeting different listener as well as renaming them

- You can mute and unmute the participant as they speak.
- During running lectures, tap on the "more button" and click on mute participants on entry so that you don't have anyone who's going to be entering the conference not to cause interruptions.
- To change controls to any participant, you can also click the arrow "^" and go to advance

sharing options where you can choose who can share, and who can start sharing when someone else is sharing, and you can change that to only the host if you want.

- To access the chat, click on the chat menu icon, and the loop bar pops up with different options.
- Then type in your conversation at the bottom of the bar and also choose who you want to send it to
- To send any files, including PDFs and PowerPoints. Along with chats, you can add different reactions [Emoji's] to other participants as they're speaking which will show on the top left of the screen,
- Now in terms of utilizing the screen, what you can do is click on share screen and choose which window you want to share or the option of streaming different files, and when you click on share, and the data will be sent over to all participants.

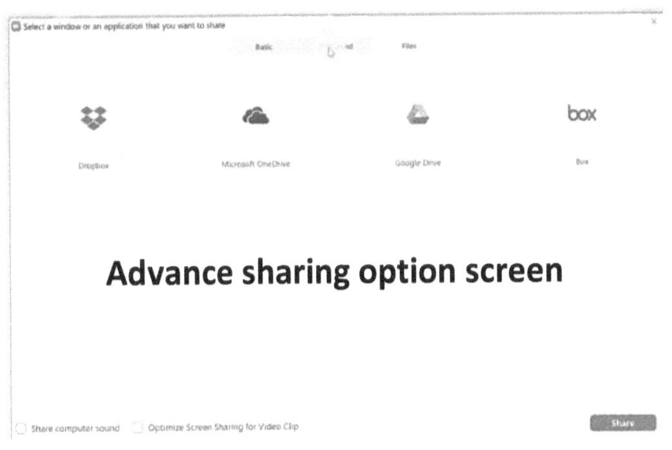

Advance sharing option screen

> If you want to save your lectures, all you have to do is click on record or press Alt + R on your keyboard and it will start recording and once you stop recording or end the meeting, it will automatically save unto your desktop

> When you are done with your meeting, click on "End Meeting" from the menu options, you can either leave the meeting if others are still discussing or you can end the meeting for all.

HOW TO JOIN A ZOOM MEETING AS A PARTICIPANT

You can join a zoom meeting in the app from your "Desktop and iOS Mobile or Tablet," dial in phone or H.323SIP room systems.

STEPS

- If you don't have the app installed yet, download it from zoom.us/download.
- To join a meeting you will need to first receive an invitation to join.

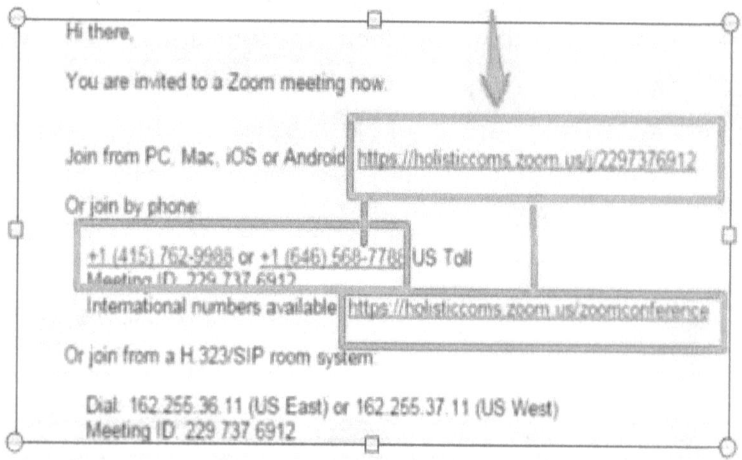

To join from PC, Mac, iOS or Android for the first time click on the recommended link, you will be taken to the zoom site where the zoom app will download automatically, install the zoom app.

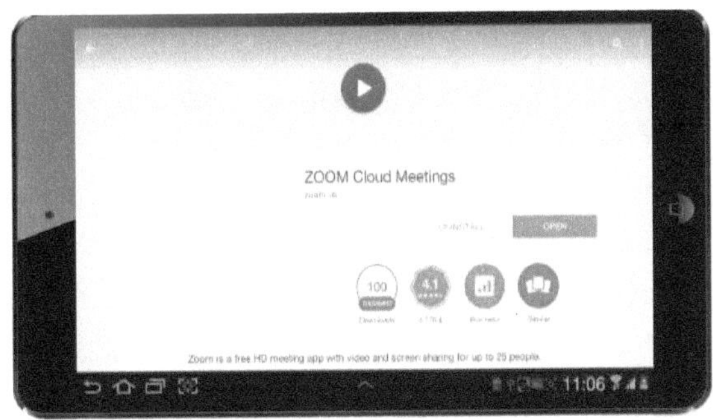

- Once you are done installing, go back to your browser and click launch application and zoom will pop up a new window where you enter your name and meeting ID and then click join.

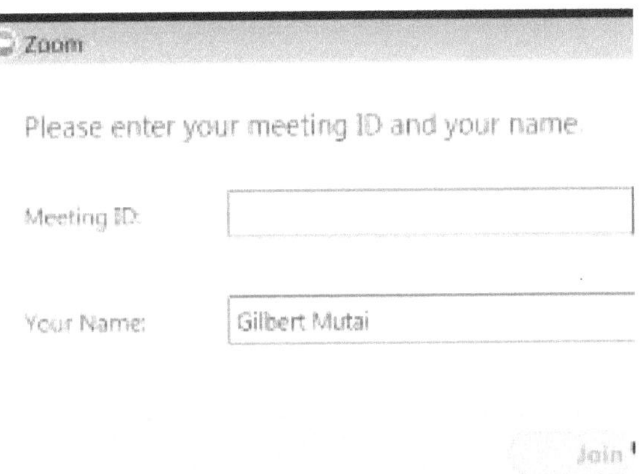

- You can also join by phone by dialing on the numbers provided depending on your location.

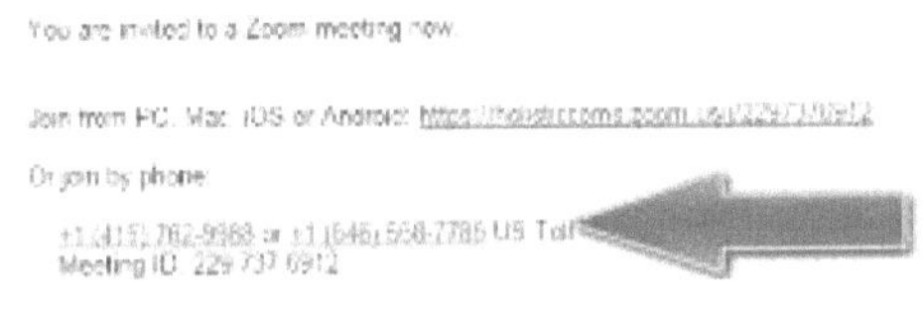

PHONE DAIL

- The same applies to an H.323SIP room system, this is used in occasions where you do not have a microphone or speaker on your PC or Mac, or you do not have a smart-phone, iOS or Android or on the road or you could not connect to a network for video and Boip computer audio
- Once you are in the meeting, select the audio option in the menu bar, your sound can come through via the computer audio or from your devices Mic and speaker
- A dialing telephone or dial out to a phone.
- Click on test Mic and Speaker to test your audio.

-

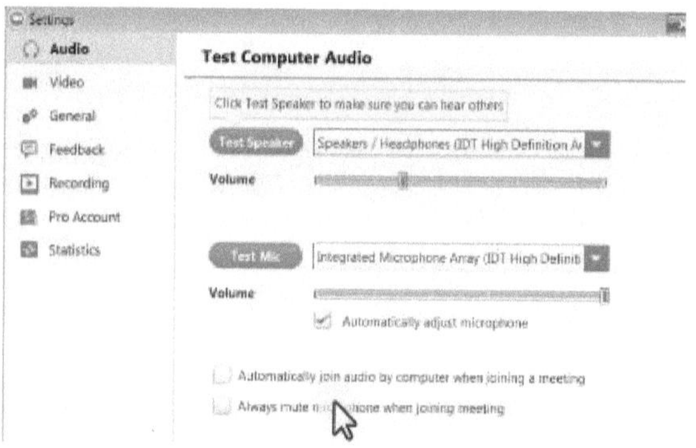

TEST MIC AND SPEAKER

- You can select the microphone drop-down and try a different audio source if the other side can't hear you and the same with the speaker if you can't hear the other side.
- Keep automatically adjust microphone settings checked.

- If you are joining a meeting from an iOS or Android device for the first time, go to "Google Play or Apple play store" to download the zoom app (ZOOM Cloud Meetings), download and install the app.
- Once you are done installing, go back to your email and click on the invite link sent to you to join the meeting
- Alternatively, you can click on join meeting on the phone app and enter the meeting ID as you received it on mail and your username to join.

JOINING ZOOM FROM DESKTOP OR PHONE WITH APP ALREADY INSTALLED

STEPS

- Open the zoom app and join the meeting by clicking "join a meeting" on the home screen/window, then enter your name and meeting ID in the pop-up window and click join.

Note: your meeting ID is a 9or10 digit number

HOW TO USE ZOOM FOR REMOTE AND ONLINE LEARNING

- ✓ Click on "Host a Meeting," to start the meeting with your video on.
- ✓ At the bottom of the Zoom screen, invite people using any of the mail options, or share your URL using any messaging platform. And you also have to share the meeting password with them to enable gain access to the meeting.

✓ To see everyone present in your meeting room, tap on "Manage Participants." Under the manage Participant you can mute them and also turn off their cameras and also mute everyone to avoid distractions.

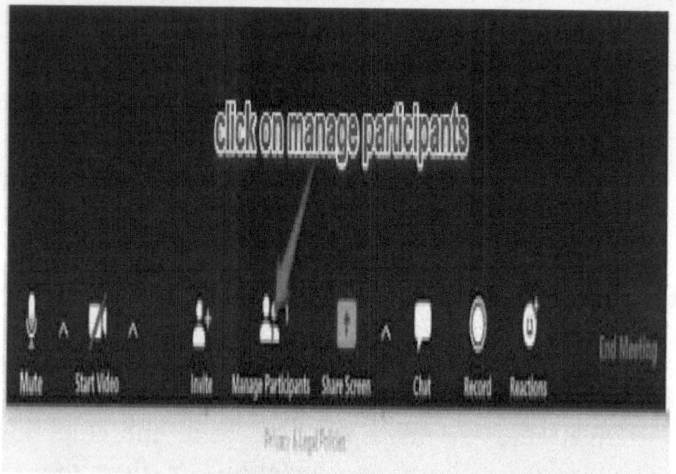

✓ You also have the option to mute participants on entry
✓ Allow or disallow them the option to unmute themselves.
✓ Allow them to rename themselves.
✓ Add sound effects or lock the meeting.
✓ In the screen sharing options, you can either your entire screen or choose which application you share, when you go to the advance options, you can either share a small portion of your screen or the sound only.
✓ You also have some files sharing options.
✓ But for learning purpose, you should open up a whiteboard to enable you to explain something, and your guest sees the white and also see you

- ✓ You can add text, draw things, and show anything you want for your online lesson. To close the whiteboard go to the floating menu bar and click on stop share, and your meetings continues with a video of you or whatever you want to show them.
- ✓ You also have the chat option/ window, which is an ongoing group chat. There, your guest or listeners can make comments or ask questions.
- ✓ You can also send a private message to anyone in your conversation. You can also send them a file or some additional options.
- ✓ They can use the record button to record the meeting, and as soon as the session ends, they'll have it download and save to their desktop as an MP4 video file.
- ✓ The reaction button allows for you or your guest to leave a reaction.
- ✓ When you are done with the meeting, go to the bottom edge of the screen and click on End meeting. You can either end meeting for all or leave the meeting.

HOW TO USE ZOOM MOBILE APP FOR FREE VIDEO CONFERENCES

Download the zoom app for iOS, Apple, or Android from Google play store by searching the word 'zoom.' When you download and install the app, then sign up to host a meeting or join a meeting.

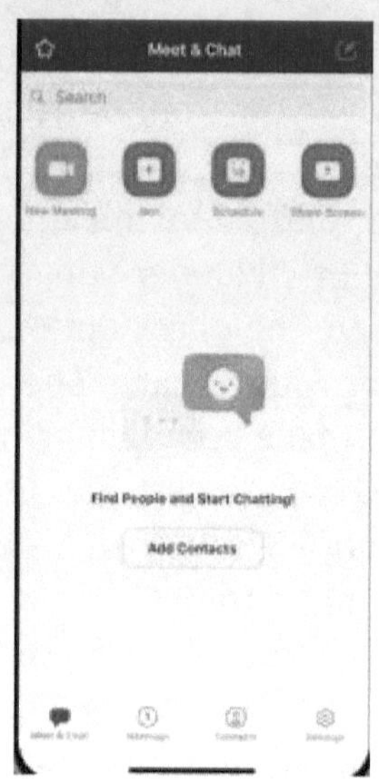

WHEN JOINING A MEETING

- On the home page of the app, click on "join a meeting," then enter the meeting ID and Meeting name which the meeting host must have sent you through email or any messaging platform in the Space provided
- You can rename to your name.
- The option at the middle of the join screen to either join with audio or video or both.

WHEN HOSTING A MEETING

- If you have no account before now, then you will have to **sign up** (providing your email address, your name and agreeing to their terms of service).

- If you already have an account, go ahead and **sign in**, and you'll be taken to the home page of the app.
- You could set up a new meeting, join, schedule a meeting and share screen.
- Press "New meeting" to host a meeting, you can start the meeting with your video 'ON' or 'OFF' and start the meeting.

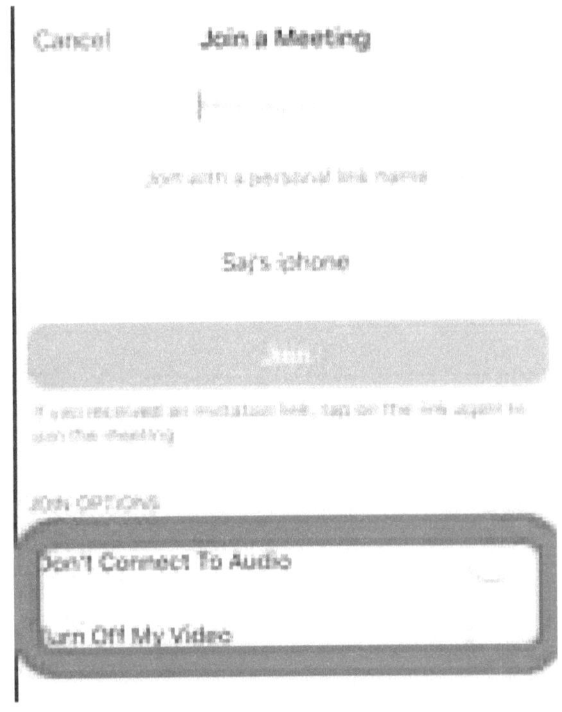

- As the meeting video screen opens, the meeting "ID and Password" will appear at the top of the screen, now share it with people in order for them to join your meeting.

- now invite some guest to your meeting; click on 'participants' at the bottom of the screen, the participants screen will pop up and at the bottom of the screen you see that you have four options " Chat, Invite,   Mute All and Unmute All". Click on "invite" to invite people to your meeting, the invite button gives you various invite options "send Email, Send Message, Invite contacts and Copy URL.

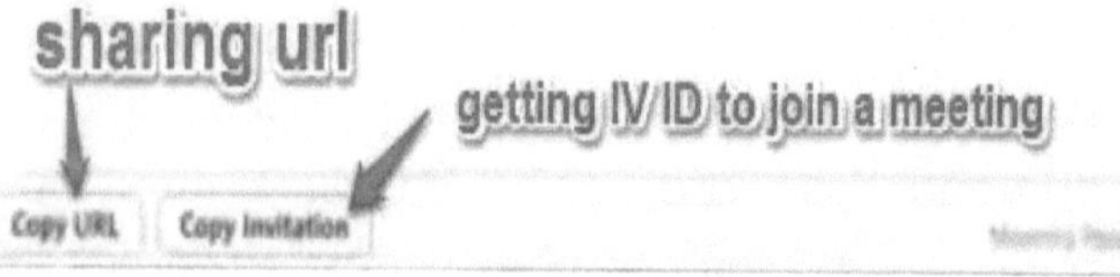

- Go ahead and stop video while waiting for your guest to join you; they'll be able to hear you as they join in.
- On that same screen, you can click on "share content" and it gives you different options of content that you can share "Screen, Photos, iCloud Drive, Box, Dropbox, Google Drive, Microsoft OneDrive, Website URL, and Bookmark".

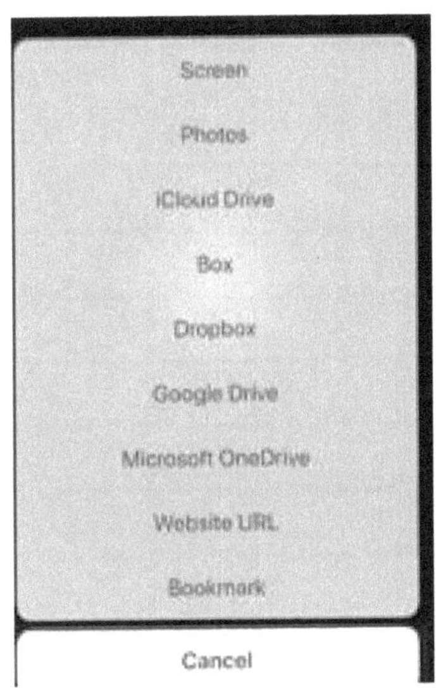

SHARE CONTENT

- Now if you press ''the more'' option which is represented as three dots [...], there's a virtual background option that allows you to change your background, and you can also upload your own photos and use them as your background

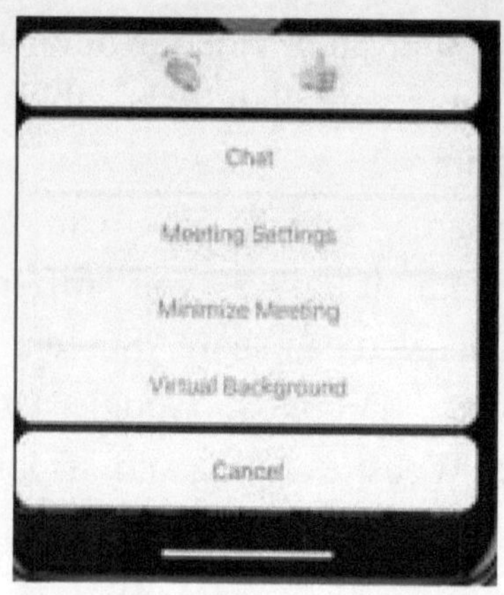

- To schedule a meeting press the schedule or calendar option and you get access to your calendar. And it is pretty easy to schedule a meeting

Meeting Scheduling Window

- When you are done scheduling press "Done" on top of your screen.
- Then you can go ahead and press your "Screen Share" option, on the share screen enter your sharing key or meeting ID: which is your meeting ID and password.
- You might also want to try the chat option, so go and click the "Meet and Chat" option and then meetings to see your personal meeting ID, send invites and start chatting.

- Under settings, you can go ahead and change some of those items from default to the way you prefer them like your meeting settings. You have plenty of options to turn OFF or ON, so scroll down.

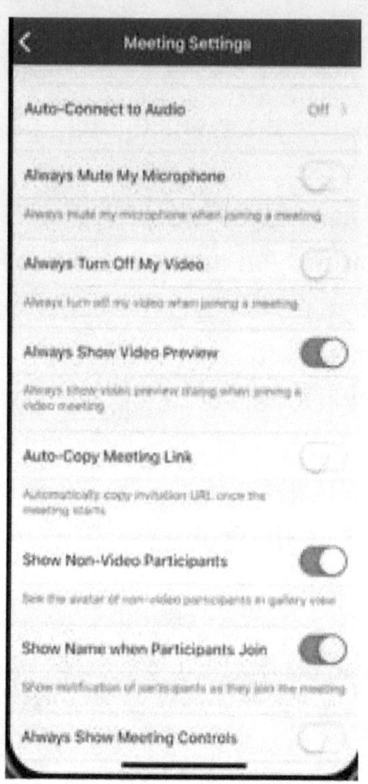

Turn Options   Off or On

When using the Zoom mobile app on Android and iOS, you can host or join a meeting. The Zoom mobile app displays the current speaker view by default. When participants enter the meeting, you will notice a video thumbnail in the bottom-right corner. You can view videos of up to four participants at the same time. If you want to see videos of up to 49 guests, you will need the Zoom desktop client for Mac OS or Windows. When the desktop app is installed on your computer, go to Settings and click Video to display the page's video settings. Then, enable the option "Display up to 49 participants per screen in Gallery View".

ZOOM OUTLOOK PLU-GIN

Aside from Zoom app downloads, it is feasible to use Zoom in other ways. For instance, there's a Zoom Outlook plug-in built to work directly with your Microsoft Outlook client or as an Add-in for Outlook on the web. This Outlook plug leaves a Zoom button right into the standard Outlook toolbar and lets you host or schedule a Zoom meeting with just a click.

USING ZOOM IN YOUR BROWSER

It is tricky to join a Zoom meeting in your browser without using the app.

You can join a meeting directly by using a Zoom web client link that appears like this (zoom.us/wc/join/your-meeting-id).

Some very skillful programmers have worked a browser extension that lets you join a Zoom meeting directly from your browser without the app's normal problems.

Zoom browser extensions

An exciting tool for quickly hosting or scheduling a Zoom meeting comes in the form of an extension for your preferred browser. There are a Zoom Chrome extension and Zoom Firefox add-on that allows you to schedule a Zoom meeting via Google Calendar. A simple click on the Zoom button starts or schedules a meeting with all the info about the meeting being sent via Google Calendar to make it easy for participants to join.

ZOOM SCREEN SHARING AND USING PAUSE SHARE

You can share your screen, whether on your smart-phone or desktop, but also pause your screen sharing. Press Pause Share when you don't want your meeting participants to watch you mess around your presentation slides.

SHARE AND ANNOTATE ON MOBILE

You can share files/docs from your phone while in the meeting and use the whiteboard feature on your phone by writing comments with your finger. To annotate while viewing someone's shared screen, select the View Option from the top of the Zoom window, and choose Annotate.

A toolbar will appear with all you're annotating.

TURN ON GALLERY VIEW

Gallery view lets you see all participants in the meeting at the same time, instead of the only speaker. To turn the gallery view on, click the tab "Gallery view" in the top right corner. If the meeting has 49 or fewer guests, you will see all their screens displayed on one page. If there are more, you'll have the option to move between pages. You can change it back by clicking "Speaker view" in that same top right corner.
On a more important call, your screen can be cluttered with participants, which becomes a distraction, especially

if your entire guest doesn't have their cameras. Hide the participants who are not using video.
Go to Settings > Video > Meetings and check Hide non-video.

HOW TO CHANGE YOUR BACKGROUND IN ZOOM

- The first click to join a meeting or create one, then below the video screen click on this arrow (^) after the video icon, from the menu list, select choose a virtual background.

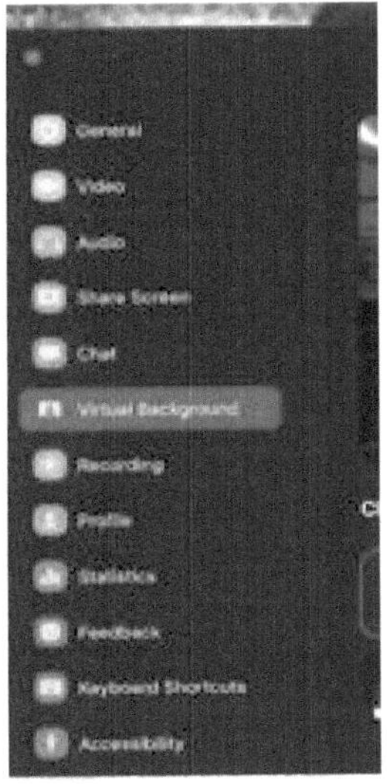

- Now in the settings the virtual background default images and video appear for you to choose from. Click on your preferred image or video then click download and the background will change.

- If you want to add your own background image or video, click on the little [+] plus sign at the right corner of the screen, select add image or video; go to the folder where you have the image or video and upload it. Now you can use that image as a background during your zoom meetings.

- If you want your video background to be very professional, go to the virtual background settings, at the bottom of the screen you will see two options ('I have a green screen and mirror my video), click on either one of the two to have a professional background.

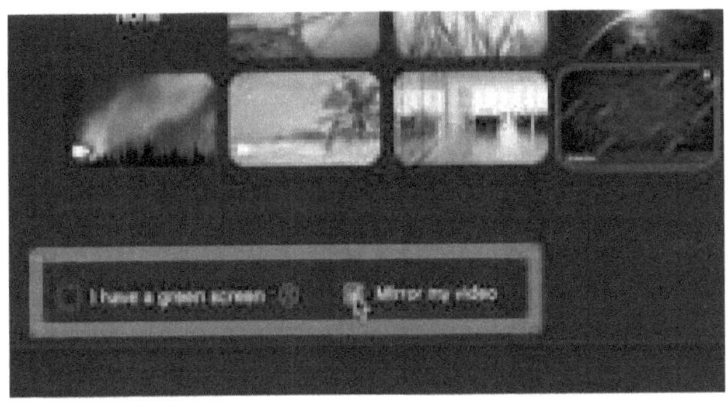

Tip: you can go to shutterstock.com to get professional images that suit your meeting place ideas for a small amount of money.

DEFAULT SECURITY UPDATES

Zoom is programmed with several security changes to help reassure users of their security while using Zoom. One of which is the requirement for a password as default for the Zoom meeting setting. This feature, combined with virtual waiting rooms, guarantees that only those people who have been invited are allowed in.

ZOOM SECURITY TOOLS

Zoom has an easy way to manage and secure your meetings while they are on-going. Zoom has various security tools you can access with a few clicks, including the ability to lock the meeting when it starts preventing others from joining, remove participants on the call, muting participants, and disabling private chats.

To access Zoom security tools, click on the security button that appears in the window. At the same time, the call is on-going or waver over a participant as if to interact with them individually -to remove them from the call.

HOW TO RECORD ZOOM CALLS AS A VIDEO

- Zoom allows you to record calls as videos. However, you need permission to do that. You will have to enable recordings in settings. You should check your account settings to make sure the recording is enabled before you get started.
- To do this "Log into your Zoom account"
- Click to view Account Settings/Meeting settings
- Navigate to the Recording tab and click video recording.
-

HOW TO RECORD A ZOOM CALL ON MOBILE

- Open the Zoom app on your mobile device
- Click to join or start a meeting
- Click the three-dot [...] menu on the bottom right corner of your screen
- Click "Record to the cloud" or "record."
- You will now see a recording icon and the ability to pause or stop recording
- Once the call is over, you'll find the recording in the "My Recordings" section of the Zoom site or App.

Where Zoom saves your recordings

- When you are recording locally, Zoom saves your recordings on the Zoom folder on your PC, Mac, or mobile device.
- You can access Zoom recordings by opening the Zoom app and navigating to meetings. You will see a "recorded" tab, choose the meeting you need, then either play or open it.

Chapter 5

ZOOM ON YOUR TV

ZOOM TV

It is feasible to get Zoom working on your TV; you can have a video call on the big screen.

HOW TO GET ZOOM WORKING ON YOUR TV

You can get zoom working on your TV by two basic means, wired or wireless.

For the wireless option, if you have an iPhone, iPad, or Mac, all you need to do is use AirPlay and Apple TV, or Chrome-cast.

STEPS FOR iOS DEVICES

- As with all Apple devices, make sure that the software is up-to-date on the iOS device and the Apple TV
- Ensure your iOS device is connected to the same Wi-Fi network as the Apple TV
- Swipe down the Action Center from the top right corner of your iPhone or iPad device on Face ID-Enabled phones that are able to execute iPadOS. You have to swipe up from the bottom of the Touch ID devices
- Tap on the Screen Mirroring
- Tap on the name of your Apple TV that shows on the list. Your screen will then mirror the Apple TV.
- Now, open zoom and start the call.
- This same process also works for Mac, and you can share to an AirPlay display; if that option is available to you, you will see the icon on the bar at the top of your screen, and then you click to share

your Mac screen with your TV, and that will get zoom into your big screen.

STEPS FOR WORKING ZOOM ON TV WITH CHROME-CAST

Chrome-cast gives a perfect bridge between a mobile device and TV. Chrome-cast dongle connects to the TV through the HDMI, giving you the means to dictate what you watch. Now, this normally is for Netflix or Disney+, but then it also supports screen mirroring from Andriod devices, Chrome browser, or Chrome-books.

STEPS

- First, you have to find the cast option; the display icon looks like a Wi-Fi logo; you will see it in the Chrome browser and other platforms as well as the ChromOS. Different Andriod devices have various names for it like "cast," "Smart view," or "Wireless projection." You will mostly find it in the 'quick setting menu' at the top of your mobile screen.
- Setup your Chrome-cast; ensure your phone is connected to the same Wi-Fi network as the Chrome-cast.
- Find the casting menu on your phone then scan for devices to share to.
- Tap your Chrome-cast, and your phone screen will show on your TV screen.
- Open Zoom as usual on your phone, rotating into the landscape will give you a perfect view.

ZOOM TO TV WIRED CONNECTION

Wired connection is straightforward.

HERE ARE THE STEPS

- If you have an HDMI port on your laptop or desktop, plug into it and also connect the cable into your TV. If your computer doesn't configure it automatically, you will have to tell it what to do with the second connection.
- If your device doesn't have an HDMI port, then you can use the USB-C instead.

WORKING ZOOM ON A SMART TV

STEPS

- The first step is to download AptoideTv on your TV
- Click on the apk, and a new tab with the installation option opens.

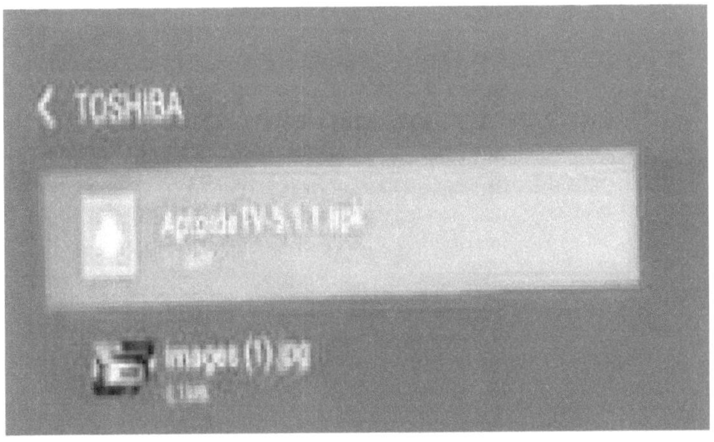

➢ Press the install tab and allow it few minutes to install and click open

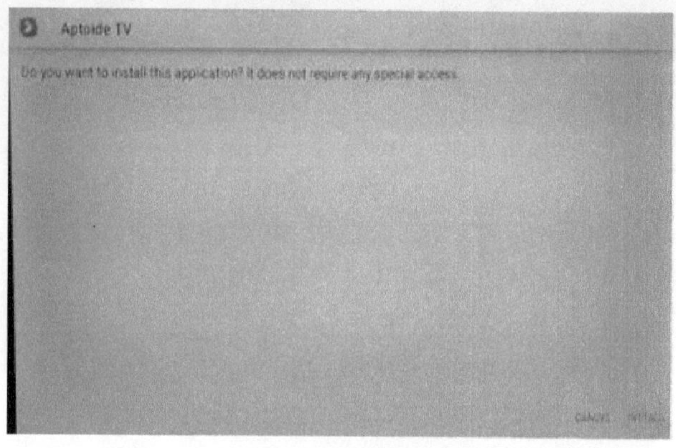

➢ In the next window that opens click "ok" and the "deny."

> Then in the search window search for Zoom app, different zoom app will be displayed for you to choose from; click the Zoom Cloud Meeting and install it.

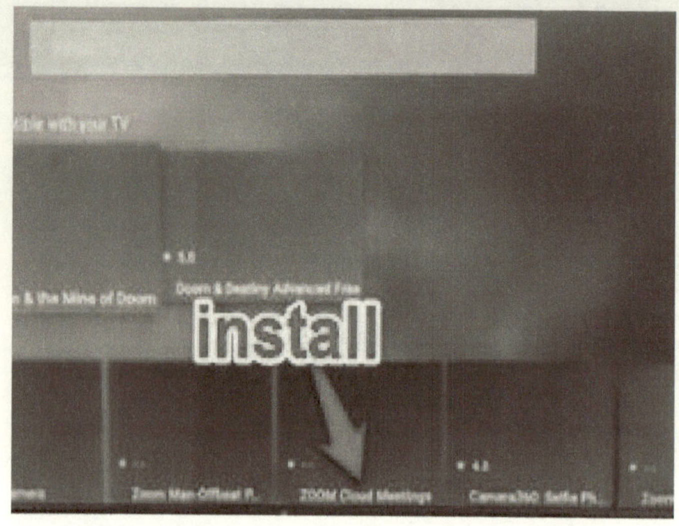

> ➤ After the installation process, open the app; this should show the zoom meeting interface or home screen.

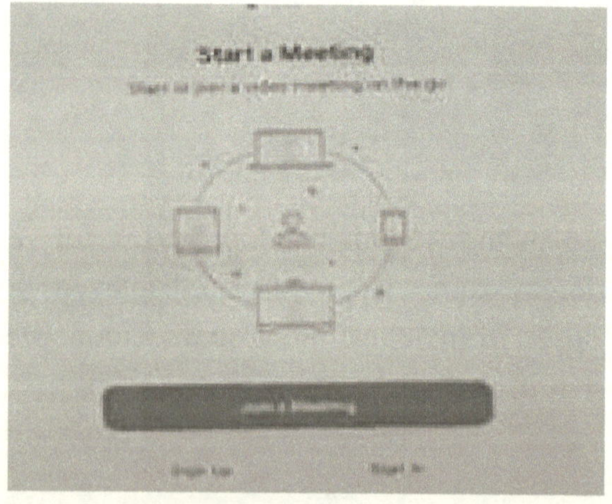

> ➤ You can now click to join or start a meeting

REPORTING OTHER PARTICIPANTS

It is possible to report participants on the call that are not welcome or are causing trouble. Also, removing them from the call allows you to send a report to the Zoom Trust and Safety team to handle such issues. This process will block them from the call now and, in the future, from interfering with others. To do this, click the security button on the meeting and then click the report.

THE TOUCH UP MY APPEARANCE FEATURE

Zoom presents the option to improve your looks when you are on a call, the feature called "Touch up My Appearance," which is useful in giving you a much better appearance when on call.

Touch up My Appearance uses a beauty filter to smoothen fine lines and look very natural. To use Touch up My Appearance;

- Go to Settings, under the Video tab; check the box next to Touch up. Or
- Click the up arrow next to Start Video. Click Video Settings, and under My Video, check the box for "Touch up My Appearance."

RECORDING TRANSCRIPTS

Not only can you record Zoom meetings, but you can also automatically transcribe the audio of a meeting that you record to the cloud. As the meeting host, you can edit your transcript, scan the transcript text for keywords to access the video at that moment, and share the recording.

TO ENABLE THE AUDIO TRANSCRIPT FEATURE

- Sign in to Zoom web portal or the app and navigate to My Meeting Settings,

- Then to the Cloud recording option on the Recording tab,
- Verify that the setting is enabled.
- Choose Turn On.
- If the option is grayed out, it has been locked at either the Group or Account level, and you need to contact your Zoom admin.

USING ZOOM ON AN IPAD OR IPHONE

- Before you start the zoom meetings, go to your camera to the selfie mode and adjust it to make sure you are presentable for a meeting.
- The first time that you'll open the zoom app on an iPad or an iPhone, it's going to ask you for permission to use the microphone and the camera as well as other things.
- It will also ask you for permission to access your calendar, allow it if you know you are going to be scheduling meetings from your iPad or iPhone so it can put the meeting right unto your calendar.
- Whenever you want to change the settings, tap on the settings and scroll all the way down, to the last option until you see the zoom app and have whatever option you want to change and turn On or Off. You should allow it access to your photos.
- You should have your microphone and camera turned off by default to cut out any background noise and distraction going on the background. To do this, go to your zoom app>settings>meetings> turn on "always mute my microphone and always turn off my video." On the same window, scroll down a little bit and turn on "always show meeting control." This feature enables you to quickly mute

yourself when you are not speaking in a meeting with the unmute button showing on your screen.

- Also, if you are the meeting host, once you start a meeting, you can mute everybody that comes in tap on more>meeting setting>mute on entry, which is a good idea cause they have the option to unmute themselves whenever they want to speak.

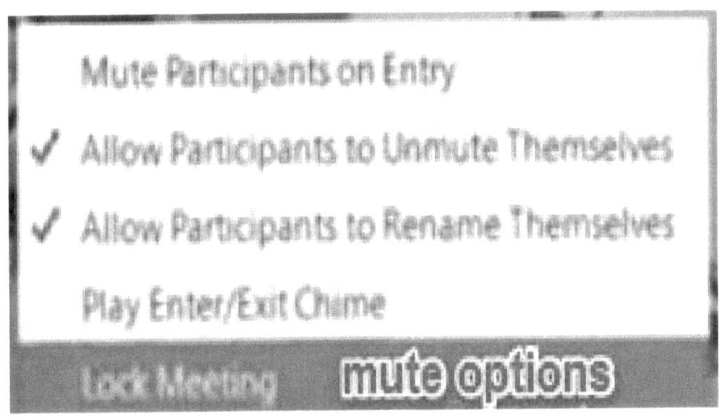

- You can also tap the participants' tab, and you can mute everyone with one button tap. You can give participants the power to unmute themselves or not.
- On the iPhone, there's a hidden feature called "safe driving mode," which provides you with a fast way to mute your microphone and immediately turn off your camera. All you have to do on the iPhone is swipe to the right, and quickly, you go into the safe driving mode, and when you are ready to talk, you tap to speak when done speaking swipe to the left.
- Now to know when somebody enters or leaves your meeting, especially when you have everyone muted, tap on the More button>go to meeting settings>play chime for Enter/Exit> turn it on. And that way, when someone joins your meeting, you'll

hear a little chime like a doorbell, and when they leave the meeting, you'll hear another different chime.

- Even when your iPhone or iPad already has a built-in speaker, you can use Ear-buds with a microphone or those wireless Bluetooth speakers or the Apple Earbud to have better audio and less distraction. When you have the wireless Earbud or the apple buds once you plug them in and have them connected, you'll see on the upper left corner that there's a little speaker icon tab and choose from the options that you want.

- When you tap start video by default, the iPad or iPhone is just going to show the selfie camera. Still, if you look at the upper left corner, you will see options that allow you to switch between cameras, this is useful if you want to show somebody a doc or something on your wall or your environment.

- When you tap the share content button, you have several options to choose from like to share your screen or photos, you can select any number of photos to share and tap done, and the images will appear on the screen of everyone in the meeting. If you tap the little pencil icon for adding annotations to the screen, you can draw right on your screen to illustrate or demonstrate something to your guest. To leave the annotation mode, click on the pencil again or tap "stop share," and you'll be back to your meeting screen.

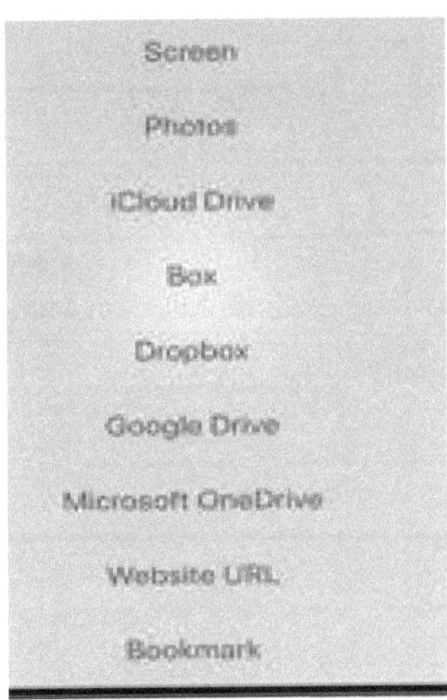

SHARE   CONTENT

> If you are sharing a pdf file, select the document and click share and it appears on the screen, you can zoom in and out, you draw a box on the screen to points out something.

> This options is only available on iPad it's called the white board option. It shows a whiteboard with different annotating options, you can draw, add text and guest in your meeting can also add their own drawing to the whiteboard.

> You can tap the little trash can in the bottom right corner of your screen to clear all the drawings or just the other participants drawings.

➤ If you click the [+] plus symbol down, it shows you all the whiteboard available to you. And you can add up to twelve whiteboard.

➤ Now if you want to save what's on your whiteboard, don't tap stop sharing yet, tap the more option and click on save to photos.

Chapter 6

USING ZOOM ON FACEBOOK AND POWERPOINT

GIVING A POWERPOINT PRESENTATION USING ZOOM

The Zoom tool can make your presentations more dynamic and interesting. Now there are two ways to do this. First:

✓ On your PowerPoint environment select insert >Zoom.

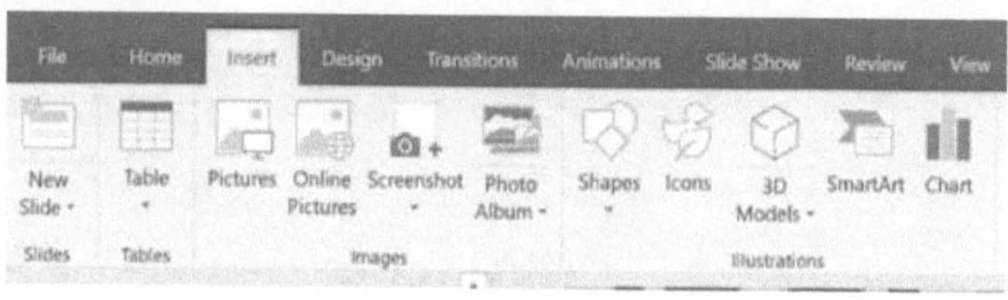

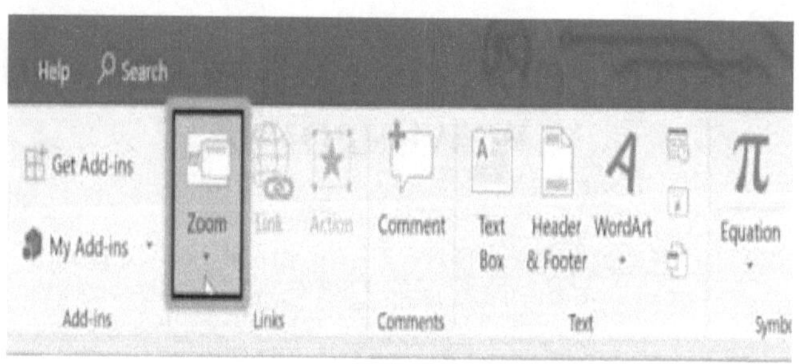

Create a summary zoom to organize your presentation into sections; this is good for longer presentations to keep your audience updated with how it is progressing.

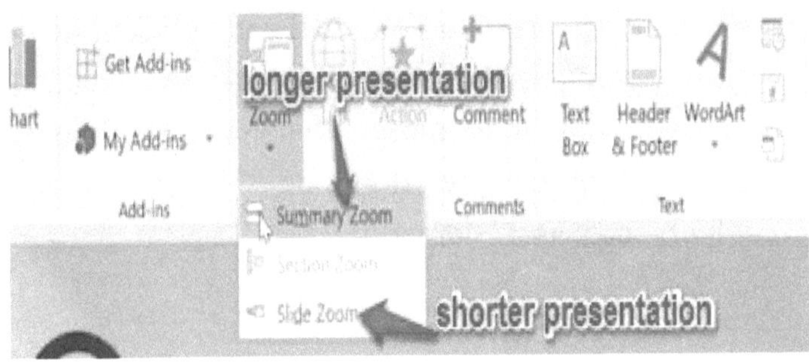
Get Add-ins
hart
My Add-ins
Add-ins
longer presentation
Zoom
Action
Comment
Text
Box
Header
& Footer
WordArt
Text
Summary Zoom
Section Zoom
Slide Zoom
shorter presentation
Comments

Media   Playback   Audio   Video   Subti
File   Home   Insert   Design   Transiti   Animations   Slide Show   Review   View
1
New
Slide
Table   Pictures   Online
Pictures
Screenshot   Photo
Album
Shapes   Icons   3D
Models
SmartArt   Chart
Slides   Tables   Images   Illustrations

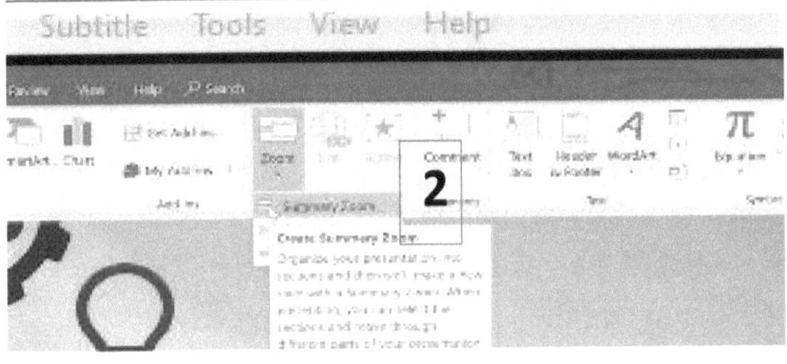
Subtitle   Tools   View   Help
Review   View   Help   Search
SmartArt   Chart   Get Add-ins
My Add-ins
Add-ins
Zoom
Comment
Text
Box
Header
& Footer
WordArt
Equation
Text   Symbols
2
Summary Zoom
Create Summary Zoom
Organize your presentation into
sections and choose which images
start each section. Summary Zoom lets
you see all the parts of your
presentation at once, and move through
different parts of your presentation.

✓ For shorter presentations you can click slide zoom. Now you can select slides to make your presentation feel more dynamic as the entire presentation can be done on this one slide only which acts as a canvas.

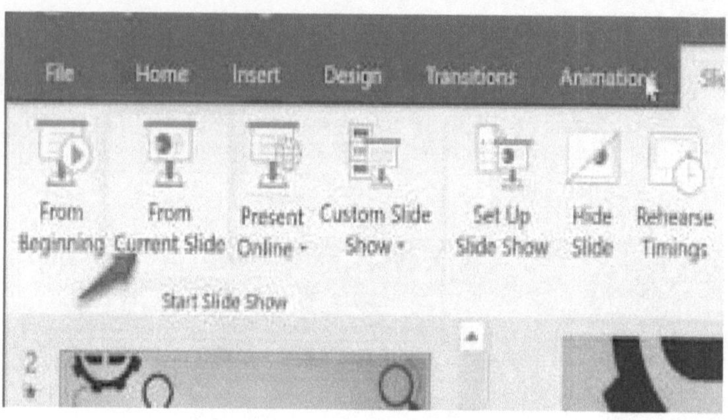

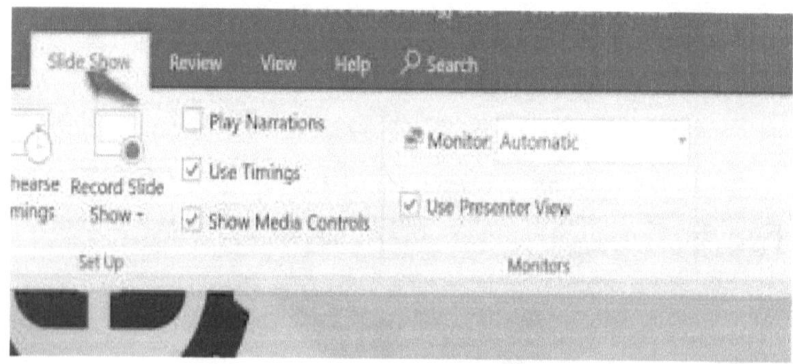

✓ Select the slides and click insert.
✓ Change to the Zoom tools format tab.
✓ Select each slide and click format>return to Zoom.

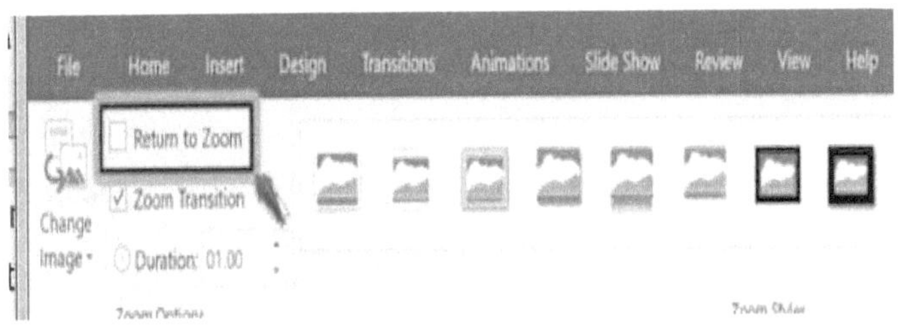

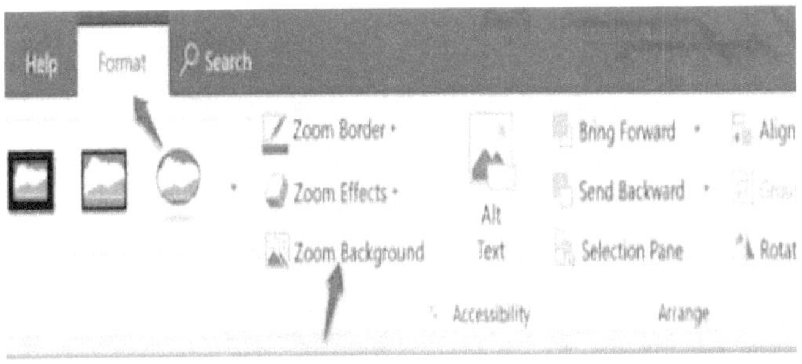

✓ You can click the Zoom background to make your slide transparent.
✓ You can move the slide around and resize them to blend with the canvas. Adding as many Zoom slide as you need.
✓ To view the slide show, click slideshow > from current slide >click inside your zoom slide to see how it works.

OR

Once you are in your Zoom environment, under the host a meeting dropdown menu;

- Select 'With Video On',   you can close Zoom's launch window. Now you should be seeing your web cam on the screen.

- If you can't see your webcam click the arrow '^' next to the camera icon at the bottom of the screen and select webcam. If your video is still not showing,   make sure there's not a red line to the video camera icon.

- Now before beginning the zoom recording open your PowerPoint or any other presentation software then click on the slideshow then setup slideshow and the then check the "presented by a speaker full screen", now click ok.

- Next, return to your Zoom meeting screen and click on share screen. In the dialogue window that appears select your PowerPoint present -ation.

- Once your PowerPoint is being shared, click on begin the PowerPoint presentation to expand to full screen.

- Now you can position your video to wherever you want on your screen.

- Move your cursor to the green bar on top of your screen until the dropdown menu appears, go to more> click on record on the dropdown menu. To determine if you are recording you can go to the green bar floating menu> more> recording; if the menu says stop recording then you know that you are recording.
- Now after you've finished the presentation, stop the recording by either using the menu buttons or the shortcut on your keyboard by tapping [Alt + R].

GOING LIVE ON FACEBOOK USING ZOOM

- **Log** into the zoom interface > click on the webinar tab> schedule a webinar. Give it a name and a description.
- **Set** the time for the webinar, the duration, the time zone, whether registration is required or not.
- Keep the video and audio Off.
- Enable practice mode, like a waiting room. Then click schedule.
- To have a collaboration video, scroll down on the window that opens after you clicked the schedule window and send them the Zoom ID.
- Now to stream live, open zoom, on the schedule page click on the scheduled webinar and click start.
- Now Zoom is going to load and ask you a few options regarding your audio and how you want to run it.

> The first screen will be the practice mode, where you can test the video and audio and set up your share screen options and even your background.\

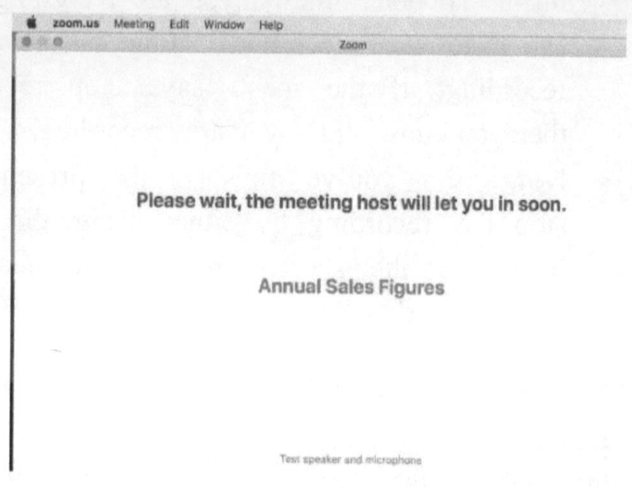

> Zoom gives you an extra option when running a webinar which is where you can go live on FACEBOOK, live on YouTube.
> Click to go live on FACEBOOK authenticate with FACEBOOK to give access to Zoom. Set the next option to be public and click ok

> Then through the wizard and click "continue"
> On the next window fill in the information required and click "Go Live." You will be redirected to zoom interface where you will hear audio sound of yourself. You can close that tab once you've gone Live.

About the Author

David Great is a tech writer and owns a blog where he writes about latest tech news and innovations. He is a geek and passionately follows latest technical and technological trends. David holds a Bachelor's degree in Information Communication Technology from New York State University.

He lives in New York with his wife Tabitha and two beautiful children.

www.ingramcontent.com/pod-product-compliance
Lightning Source LLC
Chambersburg PA
CBHW051214250726
48655CB00006B/2413